Hold
tenderly
that which you
cherish...

BOB ALBERTI

Year *by* year

DEAR ______________________________,

This book is for you. It's a celebration of who you are, where you've been, and all that you may become. It's also a book about us. The special things we've done, the moments we've shared, and the ways we've helped each other grow. Just as I see you embrace the world in your own unique way, I embrace you for being exactly who you are. My wish is that you'll read these pages and always remember that you are loved beyond measure.

LOVE, ______________________________

YOUR FIRST YEAR

1

WHEN I THINK OF HOW YOU...

MY REFLECTIONS ON YOUR BABYHOOD...

LATELY YOU REALLY LOVE...

A YEAR AGO, I NEVER THOUGHT...

ONE THING I'LL ALWAYS REMEMBER ABOUT THIS YEAR WITH YOU...

MY MESSAGE TO YOU ON YOUR FIRST YEAR...

You and love came into my *life* at the *very* same moment.

UNKNOWN

YOUR SECOND YEAR

ONE WISH I HAVE FOR YOU IS...

YOU LAUGH EVERY TIME...

I WAS EXCITED WHEN YOU STARTED TO...

BEFORE YOU FALL ASLEEP, WE...

ONE THING I'LL ALWAYS REMEMBER ABOUT THIS YEAR WITH YOU...

MY MESSAGE TO YOU ON YOUR SECOND YEAR...

...the blessedness of *being* little.

WILLIAM SHAKESPEARE

YOUR THIRD YEAR

YOU WERE SO PROUD WHEN YOU...

WHEN I SEE YOU SLEEPING, I...

I'LL NEVER FORGET WHEN YOU SAID...

YOU'RE VERY CURIOUS ABOUT...

ONE THING I'LL ALWAYS REMEMBER ABOUT THIS YEAR WITH YOU...

MY MESSAGE TO YOU ON YOUR THIRD YEAR...

You are so *infinitely* sweet.

ZELDA FITZGERALD

YOUR FOURTH YEAR

SOME OF OUR FAVORITE THINGS WE DO TOGETHER ARE...

HERE'S A LIST OF SOME OF THE GIFTS YOU'VE GIVEN ME:

ONE WAY YOU'RE REALLY GROWING IS...

I LOVE HEARING YOU...

ONE THING I'LL ALWAYS REMEMBER ABOUT THIS YEAR WITH YOU...

MY MESSAGE TO YOU ON YOUR FOURTH YEAR...

A child's world is *fresh* and *new* and *beautiful*, full of wonder and excitement.

RACHEL CARSON

YOUR FIFTH YEAR

MY REFLECTIONS ON THE BEGINNING OF YOUR SCHOOL YEARS...

YOU WERE VERY BRAVE WHEN...

A GOOD FRIEND OF YOURS IS...

AND TOGETHER, YOU LIKE...

I LOVE WHEN YOU HELP ME...

ONE THING I'LL ALWAYS REMEMBER ABOUT THIS YEAR WITH YOU...

MY MESSAGE TO YOU ON YOUR FIFTH YEAR...

Any day spent with you is my *favorite* day.

A. A. MILNE

You've changed
the shape of my days
and the size of my heart,
now both filled
to the brim with love.
Together, we've created
a new kind of life
to explore.

Thank you for
bringing pure joy
to the world.

YOUR SIXTH YEAR

I SMILE EVERY TIME YOU...

IF YOU COULD, YOU'D DO THIS ALL DAY...

WHAT AN ADVENTURE WE HAD WHEN WE...

I WAS SO PROUD OF YOU...

ONE THING I'LL ALWAYS REMEMBER ABOUT THIS YEAR WITH YOU...

MY MESSAGE TO YOU ON YOUR SIXTH YEAR...

You are the closest I will ever come to *magic.*

SUZANNE FINNAMORE

YOUR SEVENTH YEAR

I'M IMPRESSED WITH HOW GOOD YOU ARE AT...

YOU SHOW YOUR AFFECTION BY...

YOUR GREATEST DREAM IS...

MY BIGGEST WISH FOR YOU IS...

ONE THING I'LL ALWAYS REMEMBER ABOUT THIS YEAR WITH YOU...

MY MESSAGE TO YOU ON YOUR SEVENTH YEAR...

Ah, life grows *lovely* where you are.

MATHILDE BLIND

YOUR EIGHTH YEAR

8

ONE OF YOUR FAVORITE PLACES IS...

WHERE YOU LIKE TO...

YOU REALLY LIKE TO PLAY...

HERE'S A LIST OF IMPORTANT PEOPLE IN YOUR LIFE RIGHT NOW:

SOMETHING I'M LOOKING FORWARD TO WITH YOU...

ONE THING I'LL ALWAYS REMEMBER ABOUT THIS YEAR WITH YOU...

MY MESSAGE TO YOU ON YOUR EIGHTH YEAR...

Some people make the world more *special* just by being in it.

KELLY ANN ROTHAUS

YOUR NINTH YEAR

YOU ARE STARTING TO SHOW HOW GROWN UP YOU ARE BY...

A STRUGGLE YOU HAVE OVERCOME IS...

YOU'VE SHOWN GREAT SUCCESS IN...

YOU GIVE AFFECTION BY...

ONE THING I'LL ALWAYS REMEMBER ABOUT THIS YEAR WITH YOU...

MY MESSAGE TO YOU ON YOUR NINTH YEAR...

I have so much of you in my *heart*...

JOHN KEATS

YOUR TENTH YEAR

10

YOU'RE WORKING HARD TOWARD...

I SEE OUR SIMILARITIES WHEN...

YOUR IDEA OF A DREAM COME TRUE IS...

SOMETHING VERY IMPORTANT TO YOU IS...

ONE THING I'LL ALWAYS REMEMBER ABOUT THIS YEAR WITH YOU...

MY MESSAGE TO YOU ON YOUR TENTH YEAR...

The *miracle* of your existence calls for a *celebration* every day.

OPRAH WINFREY

Sometimes

I simply stop

and marvel at the

fact that you're here,

and that

you're mine.

You are a wonder,

just by being you, and

you're the most brilliant

gift of a lifetime.

YOUR ELEVENTH YEAR

YOU REALLY SHINE WHEN...

YOU CAN SPEND HOURS...

ONE IMPORTANT LESSON
YOU'VE LEARNED THIS YEAR IS...

NO MATTER HOW OLD YOU ARE,
I WILL ALWAYS...

ONE THING I'LL ALWAYS REMEMBER ABOUT THIS YEAR WITH YOU...

MY MESSAGE TO YOU ON YOUR ELEVENTH YEAR...

I'm so *glad* you're here...

RAINER MARIA RILKE

YOUR TWELFTH YEAR

I LOVE SEEING HOW CONFIDENT YOU ARE AT...

YOU SHOW YOUR LOVE FOR YOUR FAMILY BY...

I CAN SEE THAT YOU'RE REALLY MOTIVATED TO...

A SPECIAL WAY WE CONNECT IS...

ONE THING I'LL ALWAYS REMEMBER ABOUT THIS YEAR WITH YOU...

MY MESSAGE TO YOU ON YOUR TWELFTH YEAR...

You are one of my *nicest* thoughts.

GEORGIA O'KEEFFE

YOUR THIRTEENTH YEAR

MY REFLECTIONS ON YOU ENTERING YOUR TEENAGE YEARS...

THESE DAYS, YOU REALLY ADMIRE...

I SEE MYSELF IN YOU...

YOU ARE UNIQUE IN...

ONE THING I'LL ALWAYS REMEMBER ABOUT THIS YEAR WITH YOU...

MY MESSAGE TO YOU ON YOUR THIRTEENTH YEAR...

Know that I am so close behind you that if you stretch out your hand,
I think *you* can reach *mine.*

LEONARD COHEN

YOUR FOURTEENTH YEAR

YOU'VE SHOWN JUST HOW COURAGEOUS YOU ARE BY...

I SEE HOW YOU ARE GROWING UP BY...

THANK YOU FOR OUR CONVERSATIONS ABOUT...

YOU ARE REALLY GIFTED AT...

ONE THING I'LL ALWAYS REMEMBER ABOUT THIS YEAR WITH YOU...

MY MESSAGE TO YOU ON YOUR FOURTEENTH YEAR...

Love is *always* open arms.

LEO BUSCAGLIA

YOUR FIFTEENTH YEAR

15

YOU'VE STAYED TRUE TO WHO YOU ARE BY...

YOU'VE FOUND GREAT PURPOSE IN...

I'VE REALLY APPRECIATED HOW YOU...

WE ENJOY EACH OTHER WHEN...

ONE THING I'LL ALWAYS REMEMBER ABOUT THIS YEAR WITH YOU...

MY MESSAGE TO YOU ON YOUR FIFTEENTH YEAR...

Family faces are magic mirrors. Looking at people who belong to us, we see the *past*, *present*, and *future*.

GAIL LUMET BUCKLEY

You shine
brighter than I
ever could
have imagined.

You've made your life
into something only
you could create,
and your light glows
everywhere you go.

YOUR SIXTEENTH YEAR

16

SOME WAYS YOUR RESPONSIBILITIES HAVE GROWN ARE...

YOU ARE GENUINELY YOU WHEN...

SOMEONE IMPORTANT TO YOU IS...

I CHEER YOU ON EVERY TIME...

ONE THING I'LL ALWAYS REMEMBER ABOUT THIS YEAR WITH YOU...

MY MESSAGE TO YOU ON YOUR SIXTEENTH YEAR...

If I know what love is, it is because of *you.*

HERMANN HESSE

YOUR SEVENTEENTH YEAR

I LOVE SEEING YOUR INDEPENDENCE GROW WHEN...

YOU CAN'T WAIT FOR...

YOU'VE SHOWN GREAT POTENTIAL IN...

HERE'S A LIST OF PEOPLE YOU'RE CLOSE TO:

ONE THING I'LL ALWAYS REMEMBER ABOUT THIS YEAR WITH YOU...

MY MESSAGE TO YOU ON YOUR SEVENTEENTH YEAR...

There are people whom one *loves* and *appreciates* immediately and forever.

NANCY SPAIN

YOUR EIGHTEENTH YEAR

THROUGH THE YEARS,
IT'S BEEN A JOY WATCHING YOU...

I'M SO PROUD OF YOU BECAUSE...

YOU'VE TAUGHT ME...

I CAN'T WAIT TO SEE YOU...

ONE THING I'LL ALWAYS REMEMBER ABOUT THIS YEAR WITH YOU...

MY MESSAGE TO YOU ON YOUR EIGHTEENTH YEAR...

I carry *your* heart with me...

E. E. CUMMINGS

COMPENDIUM.
live inspired

Written by: Miriam Hathaway
Illustrated by: Chelsea Bianchini
Edited by: Cindy Wetterlund

Library of Congress Control Number: 2019958005 | ISBN: 978-1-970147-30-8

3rd printing. Printed in China with soy inks on FSC®-Mix certified paper.